Spiritual Rebirth-Thirst No More

By

Mayada Naami

Acknowledgements

Thanks To..........

First and foremost, I thank God for pouring into me His portion. For giving me the spiritual eyes to see, the ears to hear, and the words to speak. I thank Him for giving me the courage to step out in blind faith and overcome all the storms of life, knowing Jesus is my savior and protector. I thank Him for all the people he has placed in my life that shaped me into the woman I am today. I want to especially thank Him for my parents, my children, my siblings, my friends, and my book coach, Sparkle Smith. Without their love and support, I could not have finished writing this book.

The Lord will guide you always; He will satisfy your needs in a sun-scorched land and will strengthen your frame. You will be a well-watered garden, like a spring whose waters never fail.

Isaiah 58:11

Table of Contents

Introduction

Born one of five girls, to a strict Catholic family in a predominantly Muslim ruled country, my parents raised me in the traditional Catholic Middle Eastern way. I was six months old when we left Iraq. I celebrated my first birthday in Lebanon while we awaited our immigration visa to Canada.

Moving to Canada and growing up in a strict Catholic Middle Eastern family in a western world was complex. Even though we were Catholic, my dad was raised in a predominantly Muslim country and adopted many strict attitudes and traditions with regards to women and their role in the family.

My dad took his obligation to "marry off" his five daughters seriously. Growing up, I was never allowed to socialize with non-Middle Easterners or have a boyfriend. So, it was home, school, and church on Sundays until I was married off.

Every Sunday, I would don my Sunday best to be paraded in front of other church members. The hope was that one day I would be chosen as a wife. I did not understand this until I was almost 16 years old.

I dreaded going to church on Sundays knowing that I was being scrutinized by every person to whom I was introduced. It was less of a church and more of a "meat market."

Every Sunday I would attend Church service, which was mostly in Latin or Aramaic. Then, we would congregate in the community hall where church members would gather to socialize.

I remember never understanding the priest and having to kneel and stand whenever I was instructed to. I would kneel, stand and then kneel and stand again, wondering was this all necessary?

Chapter 1 My Story

Psalm 139:13-14 (NIV)
For you created my inmost being;
you knit me together in my mother's womb.
I praise you because I am fearfully and wonderfully made;
Your works are wonderful,
I know that full well.

After a failed engagement, two failed marriages and nine ex-lovers, I am like the woman at the well described in the Gospel of John, chapter four. My journey began in Baghdad, Iraq, in 1969, the year of the Baghdad hangings. My mother was two months pregnant with me.

On that horrific day of January 27, 1969, Baghdad Radio invited citizens to Liberation Square to "enjoy the feast." Reportedly, more than 500,000 attended the hangings. People danced and celebrated before the corpses of the 14 convicted spies (nine Jews, three Muslims and two Christians).

The three remaining Jews of the initial 12 arrested, were executed on August 26, 1969, the day I was born. Fearing the state of Iraq; Saddam Hussein's growing popularity, and foreseeing the future of Iraq under Saddam's reign, my dad made the ultimate sacrifice to save his wife and young family. Stepping out in faith, he packed only a few suitcases so he would not arouse suspicion. He pretended his family was going on vacation to visit his wife's family in Beirut, Lebanon. He left everything behind, and never looked back.

When we left Iraq, we moved to Canada. Even though we moved to the Western world, my parents kept the traditions of the Middle East. I lived a very sheltered life. We did many things with our extended family; however, I was not permitted to socialize with anyone outside of the family circle.

By the time I was ten years old, my three older sisters were married. All three sisters married cousins. In our culture, it is acceptable, even encouraged, to marry in the family to keep cultural values intact.

I remember growing up with the belief that if I waited too long, I would not find a husband. I was told that if I was not married by a certain age, people would think something was physically or mentally wrong with me.

With all these thoughts going through my mind, at the age of eighteen, I became engaged to a man I scarcely knew. He was the only son of a very wealthy Iraqi. Although his parents lived in Iraq, he was sent to Toronto in the early 1980s to avoid the wartime draft.

We hardly dated and mostly spent time together while chaperoned by my entire family. I remember thinking how strange it was to be engaged, yet never allowed to be alone with my fiancé.

In the beginning he showered me with lavish gifts. Every few weeks he came to visit me with bags of expensive clothes, perfumes, and designer watches. He told me to get my hair permed because he liked curly hair and said to eat more because I was too skinny. I wanted to please him, so I did everything he asked of me. I did not question his motives at first.

I remember an incident that occurred a few hours before our engagement party. He gave me a Swiss gold watch and left the receipt in the gift bag. When I questioned him why the receipt was in the bag, he replied that it was for insurance purposes. I suspected he wanted me to know how much the watch cost and told him so.

I said I felt like I was a possession, a doll he was dressing up to parade around as his soon-to-be trophy wife. He got very angry. He told me that any other woman would have thanked and hugged him for the watch. We had a heated argument and later that evening, at our engagement party, he did not speak to me. Despite this, I put on my happy face and acted like it was the happiest day of my life.

Shortly after our engagement, he started making decisions about our future without discussing them with me. He decided we were going to live in Toronto after we married. He was shopping for a house and furniture without asking for my input. When I questioned him, he became angry and did not speak to me for days.

This continued for a few months until one day he decided to break off the engagement. During the year after that breakup, I was hurt and confused. I did not understand why he broke off the engagement. I spent many nights thinking about the shame I had caused my family.

Because of my shame, I did not want to go anywhere, especially to church. I knew my mother was concerned that people were gossiping about my breakup. She said I must get over my fiancé otherwise no other man would marry me.

I finally gave in to the family pressure and went to church. It wasn't long before I was introduced to a woman who was searching for a bride for her son. She introduced me to her son, and we were married six months later. The marriage lasted thirteen years.

We immediately had two children, a boy, and a girl. Throughout the thirteen years of marriage, my husband and I argued incessantly. We had different views on raising our children, finances, and marriage. I wanted a partner, someone who treated me as an equal. Because of his Middle Eastern upbringing, he was very stubborn and set in his ways. When I disagreed with him, we would argue for hours.

One morning, I noticed my son speaking to his sister in the same manner that my husband spoke to me. I realized that if I stayed married, I was sending the wrong message to both my children. I was telling them his domineering behavior was acceptable. I was compelled to leave, even though I felt I was bringing disgrace to my family.

Three months after my divorce, I married a colleague of mine. I married him out of desperation and for stability. I remarried thinking it was less dishonorable than being a divorced, single mom. That marriage lasted seven years.

At the end of my second marriage, I questioned some of my family's beliefs and traditions. I was praying harder than ever and was very confused. I asked God why I was getting divorced again when the Bible says, *"Therefore what God has joined together, let no one separate." (Mark 10:9, NIV)*

In that moment of brokenness, He lovingly responded to me; *I did not choose them for you. You let them, or your circumstances choose you for them.* It hit me like a ton of bricks. I was the one making these choices. I was the one allowing my family beliefs to influence my decisions. I was not asking the Holy Spirit for guidance. My marriages were not what God joined together. They were man-made relationships.

Both my marriages were based on false beliefs. Beliefs that were passed on from generation to generation because of the culture I grew up in. I was listening to what my parents were telling me about marriage instead of what the Word of God says.

Ephesians 5:28-33 says: "In this same way, husbands ought to love their wives as their own bodies. He who loves his wife, loves himself. After all, no one ever hated their own body, but they feed and care for their body, just as Christ does the church-for we are members of His body. For this reason, a man will leave his father and mother and be united to his wife, and the two will become one flesh. This is a profound mystery-but I am talking about Christ and the church. However, each one of you also must love his wife as he loves himself, and the wife must respect the husband."

A man is supposed to love his wife in the same way Jesus loves us, the body of Christ. He is supposed to nurture his wife and take care of her the same way he takes care of his own body. And in return she will respect him. This kind of marriage is what God joins together and no one can separate.

After a failed engagement and two failed marriages, I now understand what God was saying to me. When you marry someone for worldly reasons, the marriage will not last. If Jesus is not the Rock that the marriage is built on, it will not last.

Marrying because of culture, convenience, or for security will only result in disappointment. I grew up in a fear-driven society that convinces women that marriage is the only way to happiness and security. Now I know that the only way to true happiness is Jesus. He is the Way, the Truth, and the Life. Any relationship built on this Rock will never fail.

It was my seventeen-year-old daughter who gave me the courage to divorce the second time. She was leaving for college when told she told me to leave my second husband. She said she knew I married her stepfather to provide a home and stability for my family. She told me it was my time to be happy and to stop trying to please others.

Many years later I reminded her of what she said and the impact it had on my life. She said she did not remember saying it. I believe it was the Holy Spirit that spoke to me that day. God speaks to us through our friends, family, and sometimes even a stranger. We must remain steadfast in prayer to recognize and hear His voice.

After my second failed marriage, I was broken and humbled in spirit. I felt sad, hurt, tired and disappointed. I was forty-one years old and at the lowest point of my life. After my divorce, I lost my job. Six months later, the house went to foreclosure, and I filed for bankruptcy. I was now homeless.

My life was falling apart. That is when I turned to God and was able to hear His voice. It's usually in our darkest moments when we start to pray. I prayed constantly; my heart was filled with hope even though my life was falling apart.

I kept asking God, "Why is this happening to me?" I was a loving, kind person and a believer. Then, something happened that changed my life forever...

It was the Saturday before the Lent season when I was talking to a friend about all my troubles. I was questioning why bad things happen to good people. She listened and then asked me what I was going to give up for Lent. I told her I wanted to give up control of my life. I wanted to get in the passenger seat and let God be in the driver's seat. Surprised, she laughed and said that would be hard for a controlling person like me.

I was shocked by her reaction. I did not think I was controlling. I was raised in a controlling environment, was engaged, and married to a controlling person. *How can she think I was controlling?* I will admit I was a perfectionist looking for ways to make things happen. But controlling?

The next morning, she invited me to her church. As I sat in the pew next to my friend, the pastor started his sermon by saying, "I know this is going to sound sacrilegious. It is the Sunday before Lent, and some of you are going to give up meat. Others will give up chocolate or soda. I say do not give up any of that. Why don't you give up control? Let God be in the driver's seat, and you get in the passenger seat."

I looked at my friend and she looked at me in astonishment. For the second time in nine months, I heard God speak to me. Those words were the same words I said the day before when my friend asked me what I was going to give up for lent.

Over the years, I had developed a spirit of control to protect myself from pain. I was born into a very controlled environment riddled with shame, guilt, manipulation, and fear, but that day I was reborn by the Holy Spirit and adopted by God.

In John 3:3 Jesus says, "Most assuredly, I say to you, unless one is born again, he cannot see the kingdom of God." Nicodemus said to Him, "How can a man be born when he is old? Can he enter a second time into his mother's womb and be born?" Jesus answered "Most assuredly, I say to you, unless one is born of water and the Spirit, he cannot enter the kingdom of God. That which is born of the flesh is flesh, and that which is born of the Spirit is spirit."

Like the Samaritan woman at the well, described in John chapter 4, we sometimes feel rejected and shamed by society. We must remember Jesus loves us despite our bankrupt lives. He loves us enough to actively seek us, to welcome us to intimacy, and to rejoice in our worship.

The Samaritan woman at the well had a spiritual rebirth through Jesus. Like her, we all thirst for wholeness. We seek ways to quench our thirst through men, children, job, success, family, acceptance, and addictions. These temporal things do not fill the void, and we find that our quest for wholeness continues.

   If your happiness depends on temporal things, it will be temporary. Are you thirsty? Do you find yourself alone at the well feeling ashamed; rejected by men, friends and family, or society? I have, and now I write this book to help you thirst no more.

Many of the Samaritans from that town believed in him because of the woman's testimony, "He told me everything I ever did." So when the Samaritans came to him, they urged him to stay with them, and he stayed two days. And because of his words many more became believers. They said to the woman, "We no longer believe just because of what you said; now we have heard for ourselves, and we know that this man really is the Savior of the world."
John 4:39-42 (NIV)

Chapter 2: Women of the Bible

The following is a poem from the book of Proverbs 31. It speaks of an accomplished, remarkable woman. The poet describes this woman as priceless and valuable. She has a kind, generous spirit, giving to the poor and helps those in need. She is fearless, confident, loving, smart and well respected. She carries herself with dignity and laughs at the days to come.

A Woman of Valor- Proverbs 31: 10-31 (NIV)

A wife of noble character who can find?
She is worth far more than rubies.
Her husband has full confidence in her,
and lacks nothing value.
She brings him good, not harm
all the days of her life.
She selects wool and flax
and works with eager hands.

She is like the merchant ships,
bringing her food from afar.
She gets up while it is still night;
and provides food for her family
and portions for her female servants.
She considers a field and buys it;
out of her earnings she plants a vineyard.
She sets about her work vigorously;
her arms are strong for her tasks.
She sees that her trading is profitable,
and her lamp does not go out at night.
In her hands she holds the distaff
and grasps the spindle with her fingers.
She opens her arms to the poor
and extends her hands to the needy.
When it snows, she has no fear for her household;
for all of them are clothed in scarlet.
She makes coverings for her bed;
She is clothed in fine linen and purple.
Her husband is respected at the city gate,
when he takes his seat among the elders of the land.
She makes linen garments and sells them,
and supplies the merchants with sashes.
She is clothed with strength and dignity;
she can laugh at the days to come.
She speaks with wisdom,
and faithful instruction is on her tongue.
She watches over the affairs of her household,
and does not eat the bread of idleness.

Her children arise and call her blessed;
her husband also, and he praises her;
"Many women do noble things,
but you surpass them all."
Charm is deceptive, and beauty is fleeting,
but a woman who fears THE LORD will be praised.
Honor her for all that her hands have done,
and let her works bring her praise at the city gate.

Throughout this chapter, as well as other chapters, remarkable women will be explored and celebrated. We will uncover their courage and strength despite their imperfections.

Eve - The first woman created in the perfect image of God. She was created in a perfect garden with a perfect man. Isn't that every girl's dream? She had everything a woman could ever dream of, until the enemy came into her path and deceived her. His plan was to steal her joy, kill her relationship with God, and destroy her dream life with Adam. Every woman can relate to Eve.

So God created mankind in his own image, in the image of
God he created them; male and female he created them.
Genesis 1:27 (NIV)

We all have been deceived by the enemy's lies. Whenever we feel anger, frustration, or fear we succumb to his lies. He convinces us to fight back, or maybe be passive and fall into depression.

The enemy of God does not want us, the children of God, to be happy or at peace. Why would he want that? He is called the enemy, the tempter, the snake for a reason. He is a deceiver, a trickster that takes on many different forms. He can attack you through your boss, your spouse, and even your children. By the Holy Spirit in us, we need to discern the spiritual forces of evil at work within the conflict.

When you are feeling under spiritual attack, sequester yourself in your prayer closet and bind the demonic spirits that manifest in times of conflict. We know God is not a God of confusion. He created us, like Eve, to live in a perfect place with peace, love, and companionship.

For our struggle is not against the flesh and blood, but against the rulers, against the authorities, against the powers of this dark world and against the spiritual forces of evil in the heavenly realms.
Ephesians 6:12 (NIV)

Eve was created as a partner, equal to Adam. God called Eve "Ezer", which means "help" and Adam called her Eve, which means life. God says in Genesis 2:18, *"It is not good for the man to be alone. I will make a helper suitable for him."*

Women have the power, and the enemy knows it. In the garden of Eden, the enemy of God addressed Eve, not Adam. Throughout the Bible. The enemy used women to tear down men and God used women to build men up. When they ate the forbidden fruit, Adam said in Genesis 3:12, *"The woman whom thou gavest to be with me, she gave me of the tree, and I did eat."*

God gave Adam and Eve free will in the Garden of Eden. He asked them to obey Him, trust in Him, and not eat from the tree of knowledge of good and evil. This tree of knowledge of good and evil is symbolic of the choices we make today. We have free will to choose right from wrong, light over darkness. God is Light and the enemy is the prince of darkness.

When Adam and Eve succumbed to the enemy and disobeyed God, He cast them out of the perfect garden which He created for them. He cursed the ground from which they came.

God said to Eve, because of her disobedience, she would endure pain and suffering. She would suffer at the hands of the enemy, as we often do in the world today.

Eve succumbed to the lies of the enemy and suffered the consequences. By the gift of a free will, we can choose to ignore the lies of the enemy and hear the voice of God.

God created man and woman to have joy and live together in peace and love in the Garden of Eden. God created us, man and woman, in the image of Him, perfect.

When Eve and Adam disobeyed Him, God was saddened. Any parent can relate to that. The serpent can come into our garden at any time to deceive us. He can mislead us and cause us to stray. As parents, we don't want that for our kids.

One woman's decision to disobey God caused a fallen world, a world of pain and suffering. God said to the serpent in Genesis 3:15 *"and I will put enmity between thee and the woman, and between thy seed and her seed: he shall bruise thy head, and thou shalt bruise his heel"*.

God said He will put enmity between the enemy and Eve and between the seed of the enemy and her seed. And since that day, every woman and her child are in battle with the enemy.

From generation to generation, we have been at battle with the enemy. Our children and their children will be in battle, but the enemy has no power when we choose to trust God.

When we do not choose to trust God and His wisdom we fall into entrapment. When we succumb to eating the forbidden fruit, or lean on our own limited understanding, we invite the enemy into our lives and that is when our struggles begin.

Women have the strength to say no to the enemy. We can make or break a family, a relationship or even a church or business with our choices. We are empowered to choose the light or to follow darkness.

There was never anyone like Ahab, who sold himself to do evil in the eyes of the LORD, urged on by Jezebel his wife.
1 Kings 21:25 (NIV)

Our daily choices can impact the world in a negative or in a positive way. As influencers, we can make the world a better place or disrupt the lives of others. One example is Queen Jezebel, the wife of Ahab, king of Israel, who influenced her husband to do many evil things.

She persuaded her husband, King Ahab, to promote the worship of false gods in Israel. She harassed and killed God's prophets and arranged for an innocent man to be falsely charged and executed.

Her pride and cunning, ruthless ways caused internal conflict in Israel for decades. As a woman seeking power, she sought to destroy anyone who opposed her. She is the first persecutor of saints. Jezebel was influential but used her influence for evil.

She possessed a powerful spirit of persuasion over her husband. She corrupted him, leading both herself and him to downfall and causing a curse on her family. After the death of her husband, she continued her corrupt influence as queen-mother, as her sons ruled over Israel.

Eve and Jezebel are examples of women that made choices that impacted the world in a negative way, but there are women that use their influence to do wonderful things, to trust in God and let Him lead the way.

Esther was one woman who chose to trust in God. Chosen by God to bring glory to Him, she was a poor Jewish orphan girl who became the Jewish queen of a Persian King. She concealed her Jewish origin to marry the Persian king to foil a plan to have all the Jews in the kingdom killed.

Esther was a woman of courage and bravery who took initiative and leaned on her faith. She entreated the Jewish people to fast with her for 3 days asking God to support and protect her in her very dangerous endeavor. She humbly put aside her fears of being killed. She revealed she was Jewish and asked her husband, the king, to spare her people.

God chose Esther, like the Samaritan woman, to reveal to the world His plans to save the sons and daughters of Abraham. When we completely surrender to God, drink from the well, we ask Him to fill us from the wells of living water in dry places. His Spirit is water to our soul.

It is well known that Jesus first proclaimed to be the Messiah to a Samaritan woman. A spiritually broken woman; rejected by men, by her own people and by society.

Throughout the Bible, we see how powerful women influenced kings and nations. We can see God using women since the beginning of creation. We saw Jesus speaking to a Samaritan woman, breaking all racial, religious, and gender barriers. Jesus is the Truth and Light in a dark and fallen world. When you choose Truth and Light, you reap the fruits of the Holy Spirit.

When you are in a loving relationship with the Father, you are one with God. This relationship with God the Father, the Son, and the Holy Spirit gives you the power to break free from strongholds that are keeping you from being the woman God created you to be.

But the fruit of the Spirit is love, joy, peace, forbearance, kindness, goodness, faithfulness, gentleness, and self-control. Against such things there is no law.
Galatians 5:22-23 (NIV)

Since creation, the relationship between the enemy and the woman separated her from God. The enemy is like a lion searching for his prey. Just as a lion looks for weakness in his prey, the enemy searches for our weakness.

When you trust in God and His Divine wisdom, He shields you from falling prey to the enemy. As women, we must stand firm in our faith and believe we can stand against the evil one because we have God as our protector.

Throughout the Bible, Jesus performs miracles and proclaims the power of faith. The only place he did not perform a miracle was in Nazareth, His birthplace, because of their unbelief. In Mark, Chapter 6, the Bible says He could there do no mighty work.

Jesus said to them, "A prophet is not without honor, except in his own town, among his relatives and in his own home." He could not do any miracles there, except lay his hands on a few sick people and heal them. He was amazed at their lack of faith.
Mark 6:4-6 (NIV)

Jesus healed many outcasts and had compassion for the weak. The woman with the issue of blood was untouchable and considered an outcast of society. When the woman with the issue of blood touched Him, he did not rebuke her but praised her for her faith. This is one of many examples that a woman's faith can make miracles happen.

After performing a miracle, Jesus often said, thy faith has made you well or whole. He was humble and gave credit to their faith and referred to women as models of faith. Jesus took women out of obscurity and put them in the spotlight.

In the following verse, Jesus refers to the queen of Sheba as having wisdom and discernment.

The Queen of the South will rise at the judgment with the people of this generation and condemn them, for she came from the ends of the earth to listen to Solomon's wisdom; and now something greater than Solomon is here. Luke 11:31. (NIV)

In a society where women were considered inferior, Jesus looked at women as pillars of faith. For example, the Canaanite woman pleads for her demon-possessed daughter's healing and Jesus rewarded her faith, persistence, and boldness by healing her daughter.

He scolds the synagogue leaders for rebuking the woman as she was worthy of a miracle regardless of what day it is. Jesus also refers to the woman as a daughter of Abraham, equal to a man, or son of Abraham. He lifted women up and gave homage to their faith. He drew them out into the spotlight and never treated them as an outcast or a servant.

Jesus chose to reveal He is the Messiah to the Samaritan Woman, the woman at the well. She was considered an outcast, rejected by five husbands, rejected by society because she was divorced five times and living in sin. He chose her because he knew her heart. He knew she was a faithful woman waiting for the Messiah.

Chapter 3-Spirit of Shame

Psalm 34:4-5
*I sought the L*ORD*, and he answered me*
*   and delivered me from all my fears.*
Those who look to him are radiant,
*   and their faces shall never be ashamed.*

I can relate to the woman at the well and her feelings of shame and rejection. She was a female in a society where women are both demeaned and disregarded. She was living in shame as a social outcast, representing the lowest of the low, and yet, Jesus chose her. It shows Jesus' love for the world. He had a heart for all people, no matter the gender, race, or social standing.

Born in Iraq and moving to Canada as an infant, I felt like an outcast, never fitting in, often feeling rejected by society. I was overwhelmed with feelings of shame because I was different from the other girls in school. I was a traditional Middle Eastern girl with an unusual name and a Catholic upbringing.

Jesus answered, "Everyone who drinks this water will be thirsty again, but whoever drinks the water I give them will never thirst. Indeed, the water I give them will become in them a spring of water welling up to eternal life".
John 4:13-14 (NIV)

I was thirsty for acceptance and could not quench my thirst until I met Jesus. The encounter with Jesus is one of unconditional love, truth, redemption, and acceptance. He alone is the living water that fills our void.

In so many ways, women have become parched and thirsty from pouring out their heart and soul. Sometimes, nursing the cares of the world and becoming deficit in the process. As a result, feelings of shame can manifest. After the encounter with the serpent, Eve covers herself, ashamed of her nudity. Until then, shame did not exist.

The spirit of shame stems from feelings of inadequacy. Shame drives women to hide or deny their wrongdoings. As women, we measure self-worth with how society perceives us.

*For I know the plans I have for you, declares the L*ORD*, plans to prosper you and not to harm you, plans to give you hope and a future.*
Jeremiah 29:11 (NIV)

If we fall short of the standards of society or culture, then we feel shame. It can be imagined or self-inflicted, nonetheless painful. Shame is a self-punishing emotion that causes distress and feelings of worthlessness.

I felt shame at different times throughout my life. I felt it when I was a child and did something my parents perceived as "bad". I felt it when I was a young girl and did not fit in with the kids in school. I felt it when my fiancé broke up with me. I felt it when I got divorced.

Shame is a painful feeling caused by not meeting the goals or standards, real or imagined, set by society. It is a negative self-evaluation when comparing yourself to what others think of you.

Shame can also be used in certain societies as a form of social control. "Shaming" is a technique used to stop a person from behaving a certain way. When I was a young adult, shaming was used frequently to ensure "good" behavior.

Growing up in a culture where a girl's reputation was often discussed, I heard many shame stories. I heard stories of girls that chose not to conform to the society standards. I was not one of those girls. I did not have the courage to stand out.

Shame is debilitating. It keeps you from fulfilling God's plan for you. The spirit of shame is not of God; it was created by the enemy when Eve ate the forbidden fruit. It is not a feeling that comes from God. It is a lie that the enemy tells us every time we make a mistake. God loves us unconditionally. He created us in His image. How can we ever feel shame?

He created us in love and has plans to give us hope and a future. He has plans to prosper us and not to harm us. Feelings of shame can keep us from fulfilling His plan for us.

Because the Sovereign Lord helps me, I will not be disgraced. Therefore have I set my face like flint, and I know I will not be put to shame.
Isaiah 50:7 (NIV)

Frequently, we can develop feelings of shame when there are rules or social norms, and we break those rules. When we worry about what others think of us, we feel shame. To feel shame, you must have a sense of self-awareness that others are making judgments about you or your actions.

I was a Catholic Middle Eastern girl that was very self-aware and was in constant fear of judgment. I was that woman until after my second divorce. I was that woman until my spiritual rebirth. I was that woman until I drank from the living well. Now, I thirst no more.

Naomi, Ruth's mother-in-law in the Book of Ruth in the Bible, is a woman who also felt shame. She, her husband, and sons left her beloved Bethlehem amidst the famine of Israel during the rule of the Judges. They moved to Moab, where food was more plentiful. In moving, they had stepped out of the will of God.

Not long after, Naomi had many misfortunes, including losing her husband and sons. Deep sorrow overshadowed her. She felt God had deserted her because of her desertion of Him. She felt she had deserted Him for the heathen land of Moab.

"Don't call me Naomi," she told them. "Call me Mara, because the Almighty has made my life very bitter." Ruth 1 :20 (NIV)

Stricken by poverty, and ignoring the shame, she found the strength to go back to her native land. Her heart and spirit were broken.

In the verse above, the name Mara, in the Bible, means "bitter". I know the pain Naomi was feeling. After my second divorce, I was desolate and feeling bitter. And like Naomi, I was a woman of faith who rose from the ashes of bitterness.

When Naomi returned to Bethlehem, she did not ask Ruth to follow her. To the contrary, she encouraged her daughter-in-law to return to Moab, her homeland. Ruth refused and showed her loyalty to Naomi. Ruth was a woman of courage who decided to leave her own native land and step out in faith.

Ruth was loyal to Naomi. Just as followers of Christ forsake all others to follow Him so that we can be a part of his inheritance, so Ruth followed Naomi. Ruth told her mother-in-law, your God is my God, and your people will be my people. She became in covenant with her and with God.

She had no obligation to do so. She could have left, like the other sister-in-law, Orpha. But something in her heart told her she had to follow Naomi.

In doing so, she fulfilled God's plan for her, she married Boaz and became a part of the lineage of Christ. Ruth was able to arise from desolation to copious blessings and fortune.

I can relate to these women of the Bible, can you? Have you lost everything and had to start over with nothing but your faith? Have you felt the shame of having to face friends and family after losing everything? I have, and now I write this book to help you rid yourself of that spirit of shame.

Shame shatters our dreams, turns our bright futures into broken dreams. Sheila Walsh says it best in her video "From Shame to Love." She says, "shame is not what you did, it is who you are." Shame imposes on us feelings of being something wrong rather than doing something wrong. Jesus became shame for us so we can know our Father's love. He died on the cross for our sins to be forgiven.

Fixing our eyes on Jesus, the pioneer and perfecter of faith. For the joy set before him he endured the cross, scorning its shame, and sat down at the right hand of the throne of God. Hebrews 12:2 (NIV)

He transforms our shame with His unconditional love. We are freed when we tell Jesus the truth about the things that shame us. The enemy likes to keep us in a dark place where we hide with our secrets.

Jesus is the Light that shines in that dark place. His love casts out all feelings of shame and sets us free. When you give your life to Christ, you are renewed in Him, and your past is nailed to the cross.

God is so full of grace, love, truth, and redemption. Once I surrendered control of my life to Him, I began to feel at peace, free from the spirit of shame and freed from fear, shame, and disgrace.

When I turned to Jesus and confessed my sins, He embraced me with His love and forgave me. He cleansed me from all unrighteousness.

If we confess our sins, he is faithful and just and will forgive us our sins and purify us from all unrighteousness. 1 John 1:9 (NIV)

I relinquished a need for a husband and allowed God to be my husband. After all the mistakes I made, He was waiting to embrace me, heal me, and mend my broken heart. Now, I am whole and can be in a loving relationship knowing what unconditional love is.

God's love does not rest on our personal accomplishments. It is through His grace and divine mercy that we are free from shame. He trades our imperfection for His perfect righteousness.

The Bible tells us we are conquerors through Him who loved us. In the Spirit, we are reborn and free to live in Christ. Nothing we can do can make us turn from Him in shame. When Eve and Adam hid from God, he slaughtered an animal and clothed them. He loved and protected them. This is the foretelling of the sacrificial lamb of Jesus. We are covered in the blood of Christ and freed from all sin.

Nothing can separate us from God, not even our shame. Shame is a lie the enemy wants us to believe. He tells us we are not worthy of His love. He says we are failures and that we do not deserve to be happy. He says we are not good enough, or smart enough, or pretty enough to be loved. These are lies to keep us in a dark place.

Who shall separate us from the love of Christ? Shall trouble or hardship or persecution or famine or nakedness or danger or sword? As it is written:
"For your sake we face death all day long;
we are considered as sheep to be slaughtered." No, in all these things we are more than conquerors through him who loved us.
 For I am convinced that neither death nor life, neither angels nor demons, neither the present nor the future, nor any powers, neither height nor depth, nor anything else in all creation, will be able to separate us from the love of God that is in Christ Jesus our Lord.
Romans 8:35-39 (NIV)

"Do not be afraid; you will not be put to shame.
Do not fear disgrace; you will not be humiliated.
You will forget the shame of your youth and remember no more the reproach of your widowhood.
For your Maker is your husband-
The Lord Almighty is his name-
the Holy One of Israel is your Redeemer,
He is called the God of all the earth.
The LORD will call you back as if you were a wife deserted and distressed in spirit-
a wife who married young, only to be rejected,"
says your God.
 Isaiah 54:4-6 (NIV)

Chapter 4 Spirit of Fear

Isaiah 35:4
Say to those with fearful hearts, "Be strong, do not fear;
your God will come, he will come with vengeance; with divine
retribution he will come to save you."

False

Evidence

Appearing

Real

  Fear is not real. It is a feeling created in our minds when we do not know what lies ahead. Dread of the unknown creates a spirit of fear, especially when you are battling a storm.

Be on your guard; stand firm in the faith; be courageous; be
strong.
1 Corinthians 16:13 (NIV)

Faith is necessary to overcome anxiety. In the Bible, when Jesus calms the storm in Mark 4:40, He said to His disciples *"Why are you so afraid? Do you still have no faith?"* Storms in life are troubles, trials, and tribulations. Every time a storm comes your way, God wants to see you stand strong in your faith.

He allows the storms in your life because that is how your faith grows. Miracles happen when you stand tall in the middle of a storm, knowing you have Jesus on the boat with you. Even though they had Jesus with them, the disciples were so fixated on the storm, they were afraid. How many of us know that feeling of terror when we are faced with a storm? How many of us forget that Jesus is with us through the storm?

The enemy tells us fear is real, even though it is not. Storms are real, but the fright conjured up in our minds is not. Fear is a choice.

When we listen to the lies of the enemy, we conjure up a spirit of fear. We must combat Satan's lies with the Truth, the Word of God. His Word is the only weapon we need to battle this lying spirit.

Have I not commanded you? Be strong and courageous. Do not be afraid; do not be discouraged, for the LORD your God will be with you wherever you go.
Joshua 1:9 (NIV)

When you put God first in all you do, you will not be afraid because there is no fear in God. When the Bible speaks of fearing God, it is not in reference to a tormenting fear but a reverential respect for God. God is perfect love so there cannot be torment. Perfect love casts out fear.

After my second divorce, like many women, I was afraid. I did not know what lay ahead of me. I was homeless, scared, and broken in spirit. This is when I finally turned to God.

Until that moment, fear had controlled my life. I worried about upsetting my parents. I was afraid of angering my husband or boss. I was terrified of being a single mom and a failure.

Fear immobilizes a woman into staying in a broken relationship or dead-end job. The threat of danger keeps our children home, playing video games or watching TV. They are kept inside instead of playing outside or with other children. My parents' anxiety regarding strangers kept me from enjoying sleepovers or hanging out with kids after school.

Only by faith can we enjoy life the way God intended. He wants us to live peacefully in the knowledge that the enemy has no power or authority to harm us.

We must rebuke our fearful thoughts to experience life as God intended for us to live. When our faith grows, our fear shrinks. Faith grows when we turn to God and hear Him speak. The spirit of courage is of God, the spirit of fear is of the enemy.

Before Eve spoke to the serpent, she was not afraid. She was faced with a decision to trust God or listen to the enemy and eat from the tree of knowledge of good and evil. She chose to eat the forbidden fruit, and this is when her troubles began.

There is no fear in love. But perfect love drives out fear, because fear has to do with punishment. The one who fears is not made perfect in love.
1 John 4:18 (NIV)

Trust in the LORD with all your heart and lean on your own understanding; in all your ways submit to him, and he will make your paths straight.
Proverbs 3:5-6 (NIV)

Instead of leaning on God for all things, she chose to lean on her own understanding. When we depend on our limited wisdom, we develop doubts. In a world full of uncertainties, how can we be sure we are making the right decisions? To trust in God completely means not knowing what the future holds and being OK with not knowing.

Stepping out in blind faith requires courage. Courage that allows you to be vulnerable and accept the possibility of failure. To be imperfect and love yourself as Jesus loves you.

I was forced to let go of the idea of who I should be, to accept who I am. I had to let go of shame, guilt, and fear, to embrace my vulnerability. I had to relinquish control and allow myself to be led in a direction that had no clear path.

I sought the LORD, and he answered me; he delivered me from all my fears.
Psalm 34:4 (NIV)

Consequently, faith comes from hearing the message, and the message is heard through the word about Christ.
Romans 10:17 (NIV)

The bravest thing a woman can do is to step out in faith. That's when miracles start to happen. That's when I saw miracle after miracle unfold in my life. We sometimes allow our insecurities to take over our mind, keeping us awake at night. The fear of rejection, fear of death, of being alone or not being loved, can keep us in bondage.

Trusting God with all your heart is the answer to breaking the stronghold the spirit of fear has on you. In praying and surrendering to God, you are boldly telling the enemy that you are not afraid. You are building your house on a strong foundation; for you know God is your Rock.

"Therefore, everyone who hears these words of mine and puts them into practice is like a wise man who built his house on the rock. The rain came down, the streams rose, and the winds blew and beat against that house; yet it did not fall, because it had its foundation on the rock."
Mathew 7:24-25 (NIV)

"For I know the plans I have for you," declares the Lord,
"plans to prosper you and not to harm you, plans to give you
hope and a future."
Jeremiah 29:11 (NIV)

Your strong foundation helps you weather the storms of life and protects you from the prince of this fallen world. Through prayer and a relationship with God, He reveals Himself to you and His plans to prosper you.

When you pray to your loving Father, He hears your prayers and speaks to you in the stillness of quiet prayer. Prayer allows Him time alone with you, without worldly distractions.

This is not something Satan wants to see happen. Satan does not want you to spend time with God and know the peace of God. He wants to keep you locked in fear, anxiety, and depression.

When the world tells you "No, you can't", Jesus says, "Yes you can!" When you choose to disconnect from the sounds of the busy world and make time to quiet your mind, you will hear God speak. He will quiet your distress. You will have the peace of God ascend upon you, just as the Holy Spirit ascended upon Jesus.

"Ask and it will be given to you; seek and you will find; knock and the door will be opened to you. For everyone who asks receives; the one who seeks finds; and to the one who knocks, the door will be opened."
Mathew 7:7-8 (NIV)

When you make time to read scripture and invite God into your world He will come. He is waiting for you to invite him in. The Bible says ask and you shall receive.

Ask for the power of the Holy Spirit to dwell in you and give you the supernatural power to fight the enemy. Become one with God the Father, the Son, and the Holy Spirit. Put on the shield of the armor of God and go to battle against the enemy.

We are ordained to use this power for the greater good. God gives us an abundance of talents and gifts. Many women use God's gifts and talents to love, protect, and change the world. Some women listen to the lies of the enemy to control, manipulate and bring destruction to the world.

In many cultures, fear-based ideals are used to control behavior. Growing up in a Catholic Middle Eastern world, fear was present and constant.

Finally, be strong in the LORD and in his mighty power. Put on the full armor of God, so that you can take your stand against the devil's schemes.
Ephesians 6:10-11 (NIV)

As a Catholic, I was afraid of going to hell if I misbehaved or disrespected my parents. As a Middle Eastern girl, I feared bringing shame to my family if I didn't follow the Middle Eastern traditions.

My parents were frightened that I would be led astray by my non-Middle Eastern friends. I could speak to non-Middle Easterners but discouraged from developing a close relationship with them.

Still today, many children are not allowed to socialize with other children because of the color of their skin or their parents' religious backgrounds.

The unease of "different" creates division among Blacks and Whites, Jews and Christians, Christians and Muslims, Americans, and non-Americans. When we accept one another and stand united as children of God, the world will be a kinder place.

I was guilty of making the same mistakes when I became a parent. I stressed about the unknown. I didn't allow my daughter to spend the night at any of her friend's house. However, her friends were welcome to stay at our home. Of course, because of my fearfulness, she did not have many friends.

This is just one example of how I allowed my anxiety to make decisions that were not in the best interest of my family. I also recall an incident when my son was sick, that I let worry take control of me.

During his hospital stay, I remember him telling me that my concern for his health was causing him anxiety and distress. I reflected on it when he told me this.

I prayed and surrendered my son's health to God. I reminded myself that he is a child of God, and I was just the vessel that brought him into the world.

I remember the spirit of peace that came over me after I surrendered. I prayed and said to God, "He is your child. I give him to You, and I trust Your Will for my son." Our children do not belong to us. They belong to Him, the creator of the universe.

During their adolescent years, I wasted too much time worrying and causing myself and them unnecessary stress. Before they left the nest, I should have trusted God and enjoyed the precious time we had together. I could have spent more time loving them, not fearing for them.

We are blessed with children; to love and cherish them for the time that we have together. I regret not realizing it sooner.

Chapter 5- Spirit of Control

Romans 16:18
For those who are such do not serve our Lord Jesus Christ, but their own belly, and by smooth words and flattering speech deceive the hearts of the simple.

A manipulative spirit is a spirit that seeks to control people, situations, or outcomes. People that control others do so because their own life is out of control.

A person influenced by a spirit of manipulation will make you feel guilty that you aren't doing enough. I was in a relationship with that person, that person was me. I developed a spirit of control and manipulation after being hurt by people who I trusted to protect me.

I came to understand this recently after watching a YouTube video. It was early 2019, shortly after moving into my new home in Dallas. My daughter invited me to watch a video she came across on YouTube. It was a 2011 video called "Stop Tolerating the Jezebel" by Pastor Robert Morris. (Coincidentally, she did not know I attend service at Gateway Church and Pastor

Morris is the Senior Pastor. I call these moments a "God- incidence", not a coincidence.)

In the video, Pastor Robert says the problem with a Jezebel spirit is we do not want to confront it because of what we will get back. I realized that's how I felt about many people in my life. I am certain that, at times, my kids felt that way about me.

There are moments in our lifetime where we have been controlling or controlled. Pastor Morris said, if there is someone you dread confronting, it is very possible a Jezebel spirit is present. You dread either the over-the-top reaction you will get, or the rejection or withdrawal you will get. When you allow this, you may be tolerating a Jezebel spirit.

Pastor Morris lists six characteristics of a Jezebel spirit: insecurity, rejection, pride, arrogance, manipulation, and control. He says it is a manipulating, controlling, insecure, jealous spirit.

It's born of insecurity and rejection, and it becomes manipulating and controlling. His words struck me. I realized I had, at times in my life, tolerated a Jezebel spirit.

It made complete sense to me. As a child I was very insecure and often felt rejected. This led me to become controlling and manipulative.

I was trying to control and manipulate people and situations to protect myself from further pain or rejection. I was influenced by the spirit of control and manipulation when I wanted things a certain way.

I was controlling and manipulating my circumstances to protect my children from pain and suffering. In the end, I caused myself and them more pain and suffering. Now, I ask myself: *is this God's will or my will?*

When it's God's will for my life, I have peace. After years of doing things according to my will, I have learned to be still and wait for His perfect plan for me.

Sometimes what you make happen is not in line with God's plan for you. You may try to manipulate and control your circumstances only to realize that you messed up or missed out on your blessing.

He says, "Be still, and know I am God."
Psalm 46:10

You will not have peace until you surrender to God. I finally have peace in my life when I take a step back and say: *Lord I know I can make things happen, but I will wait on You, and Your perfect will for me.*

The manipulative Jezebel spirit will try to convince you that you must do something or else you won't get what you want.

The person with this spirit relies on fear and guilt to control other people's actions. Sometimes, it is so subtle you don't notice you are manipulating or are being manipulated.

I was very good at being subtle. I convinced myself I was doing the right thing, for the right reasons. I wanted things perfect, so I always had to be in control.

No matter the reason, it is never ok to try to control or manipulate a person or a situation. God did not create us to dominate others. That is the work of the enemy.

The enemy convinces us that we must dominate someone to have control of them or the situation. We must resist the cunning way of the serpent.

Some try to control people because of their fear of rejection or abandonment. A person with insecurities may become controlling because of low self-esteem, creating a false positive sense of self.

The enemy tried to manipulate Jesus when he was in the desert for forty days, but Jesus resisted. Jesus fought back with Scripture and that is what we must do.

Jesus often went away to spend time alone with God. Solitude can benefit us greatly when we use that time to sort through, with our Father, whatever is on our minds and in our hearts.

When the enemy tempted Eve to eat the forbidden fruit and be like God, he used manipulation to convince her. He said to her, *"You will not surely die. For God knows that in the day you eat of it, your eye will be opened. And you will be like God, knowing good and evil."* He used lies and deception to manipulate Eve into disobeying God.

But I am afraid that just as Eve was deceived by the serpent's cunning, your minds may somehow be led astray from your sincere and pure devotion to Christ.
2 Corinthians 11:3 (NIV)

Like the serpent in the garden of Eden, there are people that lie to us, to influence our decisions for their own personal gain. We must be diligent in recognizing this manipulating spirit and must rebuke the spirit in the name of Jesus.

We cannot override the wisdom of God. Before you make any decision, you must ask God: *Lord, tell me where I should go, what I should do.* In seeking God's wisdom, you open the door to Him and invite Him into your home and your life.

Today, when I notice I am manipulating a situation, I decide to step back and wait on God. The decision to wait on Him has given me peace. You will experience this peaceful feeling when you give up your controlling nature. It is so exhausting trying to control every situation and outcome.

I was trying so hard to control all aspects of my life that I rarely accomplished anything. I felt like a caged hamster spinning on a wheel and not really getting anywhere. I started to accomplish great things when I let go of fear and rebuked my spirit of control.

All my past trials and tribulations stemmed from making decisions to manipulate and control my circumstances. It's become easier to relinquish control since trusting in God has resulted in many blessings.

It has been ten years since I gave up control of my life and asked Jesus to take the wheel. Sometimes, I still catch myself trying to manipulate the outcome, for fear of failure. Thankfully, I recognize it and rebuke the spirit of fear.

Fear can manifest itself as control and manipulation. If we tolerate the Jezebel spirit, in ourselves or others, it can destroy our lives.

For example, when a man fears his wife is cheating, he begins to control and dictate what she can and cannot do; where she goes and how she dresses. When a woman fears her children will make the wrong decisions, she will try to control their behavior with fear of punishment.

These are just a few examples of how a spirit of control can make people do things that can hurt the ones they love.

I was controlling because I wanted things to be perfect. My idea of perfect and God's perfect plan for me were not the same.

Perfect love casts out all fear. His love is perfect. Nothing in this world is perfect or will ever be perfect. Accepting that was my first step in my salvation. I have learned to completely trust Him and be secure in Him. Everything else is imperfect.

There is no fear in love. But perfect love drives out fear, because fear has to do with punishment. The one who fears is not made perfect in love.
1 John 4:18 (NIV)

Chapter 6- Spirit of Love

1 Corinthians 13:4-7
Love is patient, love is kind. It does not envy, it does not boast, it is not proud. It does not dishonor others, it is not self-seeking, it is not easily angered, it keeps no record of wrongs. Love does not delight in evil but rejoices with the truth. It always protects, always trusts, always hopes, always perseveres.

This verse is one of the most popular verses in the Bible, especially used in wedding ceremonies. Love, described in the Bible, is patient, kind, humble, respectful, and forgiving, not jealous, angry, selfish, or mean. Love is trusting, hopeful and forever. God is Love.

This kind of love is called Agape love. Agape love is God's perfect, unconditional love for His children. The promise of love and salvation was fulfilled through Jesus Christ, who died for us so we can be reborn in Him.

But the fruit of the Spirit is love, joy, peace, forbearance, kindness, goodness, faithfulness, gentleness and self-control.
Galatians 5:22-23 (NIV)

Dear friends, let us love one another, for love comes from God. Everyone who loves has been born of God and knows God. Whoever does not love does not know God, because God is love.
1 John 4:7-8 (NIV)

In today's modern world, the concept of love is mostly idealized as romantic love. The truest and highest form of love is when the presence of God is within each of us.

Love is one of the fruits of the Holy Spirit. As described in Galatians 5 verse 22, love naturally expresses itself when you have the Holy Spirit dwelling in you. When the Spirit dwells in you, you shine with love, joy, and peace. You are patient, kind, good, gentle, and manifest self-control.

The Bible says without love you gain nothing. If you have faith without love, you are nothing. One must love God above all. Secondly, you must love one another and forgive each other, the way Jesus loves and forgives you.

In the same way, let your light shine before others, so that they may see your good works and give glory to your Father who is in heaven.
Mathew 5:16

If I speak in the tongues of men or of angels, but do not have love, I am only a resounding gong or a clanging cymbal. If I have the gift of prophecy and can fathom all mysteries and all knowledge, and if I have a faith that can move mountains, but do not have love, I am nothing. If I give all I possess to the poor and give over my body to hardship that I may boast, but do not have love, I gain nothing.
1 Corinthians 13:1-3 (NIV)

Shortly after I surrendered my life to God, I came under spiritual attack. I was recently divorced and had a heart for Christ. In the divorce, I had lost everything except my children. That's when the enemy came after my children.

At first, I didn't realize what was happening and why. I questioned why terrible things were happening to my kids. A friend and brother in Christ explained to me the reason I was under spiritual attack. The enemy likes to attack, especially after you surrender your life to Christ.

After my second divorce, all I had left was my kids. The enemy knew my weakness. My faith was being tested, like Job in my favorite Bible story.

In the book of Job, Job was a wealthy man who found favor with God because of his virtuous and righteous ways. Interestingly, God is bragging to Satan about Job. Satan then responds by saying that Job is only righteous because God has favored him generously. Satan then challenges God saying, if God allowed him to inflict pain and suffering; Job will change and curse God. God permits Satan to abuse Job, but he forbids Satan to take Job's life.

In times of trouble, we question why things happen and if God exists. It is not God who makes bad things happen, it is the enemy. The enemy wants you to doubt your faith and God's love for you. He wants you to turn from God and curse God.

Some people turn away from God. They doubt God's existence during difficult times in their life. They question why God, if He exists, would let bad things happen.

Job's love for God never wavered. Over the course of one day, Job is informed that his sheep, servants, and ten children have all died. Then Job is tormented with painful skin sores. His wife tells him to denounce God, but Job's love for God never ceases.

Even through his sorrow, grief, and pain, he praises God. Because of Job's love for God, God restored Job's health, doubled his previous wealth, gave him more children and he lived a very long life.

We must love God with all our hearts to withstand the attack of the enemy. We must surrender our home, children, money, and belongings to God. When these things are second to God, the enemy cannot manipulate us into submission.

Satan loses his hold on you when your love for God is greater than your love for anyone or anything in this world. When you love God above all else, you walk in dominion over these spirits.

God knows our weakness but so does the enemy. The enemy will find the rabbit hole in your weakness and get in. If the enemy sees you love someone more than you love God, he will find a way to attack you through that relationship. Your love for God is your protection against the evil, scheming one.

In the Old King James Version Bible, the word love is mentioned 310 times. The greatest of all things is love. How simple, but true it is.

"The most important one," answered Jesus, "is this: 'Hear, O Israel: The Lord our God, the Lord is one. Love the Lord your God with all your heart and with all your soul and with all your mind and with all your strength.' The second is this: 'Love your neighbor as yourself.' There is no commandment greater than these."
Mark 12:29-31

In Mark 12:29-31, Jesus says your love for God is the most important commandment of all, and to love yourself and others is the second most important. No other commandment is greater than these.

When you have love in your heart, even towards your enemy, you find peace in a world full of hate. Love is an action verb that inspires and impacts all our relationships. I choose to manifest love in my words and actions every day.

When you do everything in the name of love, your light will shine, and you will make this world a better place. When the world leaves you high and dry, come to the well, and let Jesus fill you up with love beyond measure.

Here are some Bible verses to fill your love tank:
(All verses are NIV)

Be completely humble and gentle; be patient, bearing with one another in love. Make every effort to keep the unity of the Spirit through the bond of peace.
Ephesians 4:2-3

Above all, love each other deeply, because love covers over a multitude of sins.
1 Peter 4:8

Dear friends, since God so loved us, we also ought to love one another.
1 John 4:11

And he has given us this command: Anyone who loves God must also love their brother and sister.
1 John 4:21

And over all these virtues put on love, which binds them all together in perfect unity.
Colossians 3:14

Dear friends, let us love one another, for love comes from God. Everyone who loves has been born of God and knows God. Whoever does not love does not know God, because God is love.
1 John 4:7

We love because he first loved us.
1 John 4:19

And now these three remain: faith, hope and love. But the greatest of these is love.
1 Corinthians 13:13

This is how we know what love is: Jesus Christ laid down his life for us. And we ought to lay down our lives for our brothers and sisters. If anyone has material possessions and sees a brother or sister in need but has no pity on them, how can the love of God be in that person? Dear children, let us not love with words or speech but with actions and in truth.
1 John 3:16-18

Love must be sincere. Hate what is evil; cling to what is good. Be devoted to one another in love. Honor one another above yourselves.
Romans 12:9-10

Let no debt remain outstanding, except the continuing debt to love one another, for whoever loves others has fulfilled the law.
Romans 13:8

"As the Father has loved me, so have I loved you. Now remain in my love. If you keep my commands, you will remain in my love, just as I have kept my Father's commands and remain in his love."
John 15:9-10

For God so loved the world that he gave his one and only Son, that whoever believes in him shall not perish but have eternal life.
John 3:16

This is how God showed his love among us: He sent his one and only Son into the world that we might live through him. This is love: not that we loved God, but that he loved us and sent his Son as an atoning sacrifice for our sins. Dear friends, since God so loved us, we also ought to love one another. No one has ever seen God; but if we love one another, God lives in us and his love is made complete in us.
1 John 4:9-12

And so, we know and rely on the love God has for us. God is love. Whoever lives in love lives in God, and God in them. This is how love is made complete among us so that we will have confidence on the day of judgment: In this world we are like Jesus. There is no fear in love. But perfect love drives out fear, because fear has to do with punishment. The one who fears is not made perfect in love.
1 John 4:16-18

"My command is this: Love each other as I have loved you. Greater love has no one than this: to lay down one's life for one's friends."
John 15:12-13

Now therefore that the LORD your God is God, the faithful God who keeps covenant and steadfast love with those who love him and keep his commandments, to a thousand generations.
Deuteronomy 7:9

A friend loves at all times, and a brother is born for a time of adversity.
Proverbs 17:17

But you, Lord, are a compassionate and gracious God, slow to anger, abounding in love and faithfulness.
Psalms 86:15

But God demonstrates his own love for us in this: While we were still sinners, Christ died for us.
Romans 5:8

But because of his great love for us, God, who is rich in mercy, made us alive with Christ even when we were dead in transgressions- it is by grace you have been saved.
Ephesians 2:4-5

See what great love the Father has lavished on us, that we should be called children of God! And that is what we are! The reason the world does not know us is that it did not know him.
1 John 3:1

Love does no harm to a neighbor. Therefore, love is the fulfillment of the law.
Romans 13:10

Do everything in love.
1 Corinthians 16:14

Many claim to have unfailing love, but a faithful person who can find? The righteous lead blameless lives; blessed are their children after them.
Proverbs 20:6-7

Chapter 7- I am Woman

In this final chapter, we will be exploring the lives of influential woman who have paved the way for us today. These victors, leaders, and heroines used their God-given talents to change the course of history. They are women of strength, courage, and determination. Some of them are women from the Bible, and some are modern-day trailblazers.

Woman, since the beginning of time, have been used by God to fulfill His plan for His chosen people. In contrast, the enemy will try to use the power of God's women to destroy God's men.

Sarah, wife of Abraham, was chosen to be the mother of Isaac. She was childless until she was 90 years old. God had promised Abraham that Sarah would be "a mother of all nations" (Genesis 17:16) and that she would conceive and bear a son, but Sarah did not believe. She lost patience which led her to influence Abraham to sleep with his servant, Hagar, an Egyptian slave. Hagar bore him a son which started a conflict that continues today.

Miriam, sister of Moses, played an important role in the exodus of the Jewish people from Egypt. She convinced Pharaoh's daughter to keep Moses and raise him. The Pharoah tried to use the Jewish midwives to kill all the firstborn sons, which included Moses. In Exodus 1:17, the Bible says the midwives, Shiphrah and Puah, refused because they feared God and did not do as the king of Egypt commanded them. Like the midwives, we must stand together, united against the enemy and his plans to kill, steal, and destroy.

The wise woman builds her house, but with her own hands the foolish one tears hers down.
Proverbs 14:1 (NIV)

Mary Magdalene

Another example of courage and faithful devotion to Christ is Mary Magdalene. Mary Magdalene was an apostle who followed and financially supported Jesus' ministry. She was possessed with seven demons. She was the first account of Jesus' ministry of deliverance and was his first miracle.

Mary Magdalene is referred to as the "apostle to the apostles." When I was a baby, I was baptized and given her name as my baptismal namesake. I grew up thinking I was named after a repentant prostitute. This widespread belief was a misconception that started in the year 591. Pope Gregory I confused Mary Magdalene with the promiscuous woman from Luke chapter 7.

This is a perfect example of how the world can misjudge a person based on false assumptions. In 1969, the confusion was cleared and removed from the General Roman Calendar, but many to this day still have this wrong notion of Mary Magdalene.

Since the early Christian movement, women were regarded as inferior. The fact that Mary Magdalene was mentioned throughout the Bible indicates that she was vital to Jesus' ministry. She was the first to see the empty tomb and the first to see Him resurrected.

She was faithful and strong. Jesus cast out her demons, restored her strength, and gave her the power to spread His Word.

He respected and understood the important and influential role of women. He gave Mary Magdalene a leading role in a society where women were regarded as weak. He elevated her to a position of great honor and respect.

Today, like Mary Magdalene, He heals us and calls us to ministry to use the gifts He has given us to help and bless others. No matter what demons are in your past, you too can follow Christ and use your talents to minister to others.

Katie Luther

Katie Luther, born Katharina von Bora, is also a woman who dedicated her life to helping and serving others. At age nine she entered the convent and by age sixteen, she "took the veil" in marriage to Christ. In 1523, after reading Martin Luther's writings, she and eleven of her nun friends decided to leave the convent.

In those days it was unheard of, it was against the law. She wrote Martin Luther a letter and requested his help to escape the convent. She told him she and her friends did not want to go along with the Roman Catholic church's doctrine and wanted to hear more of his teachings.

At the time Martin Luther was rejecting several teachings and practices of the Roman Catholic Church. On Easter Eve, Katie and the eleven nuns escaped the convent with the help of a man who was delivering fish to the convent.

He delivered the fish and then loaded the twelve nuns into the empty barrels. After the nuns arrived in

Wittenberg, Martin Luther arranged for some of the nuns to wed.

Katie was feisty for the times, and Martin had trouble finding her a husband. After several failed attempts, he wed her. She was twenty-six and he was forty-two.

Martin and Katie had a powerful relationship. They were married for twenty-one years until his death in 1546. She worked with Martin as partners in his ministry, handling all the household affairs while raising their six children and other orphaned children.

She farmed, fished, and ran a brewery to provide for their family. She housed refugees from across Europe and ministered to the sick and poor. Katie was a woman of valor, as described in Proverbs 31. She partnered with her husband to take care of her family and the community.

During the Bubonic Plague of 1527, Katie operated a hospital on-site with other nurses. She exemplifies the virtuous woman described in Proverbs 31. Martin trusted her in everything and when he died, he left her his entire inheritance, which was unusual at that time.

Katie Luther was a strong, confident, and determined woman with a heart for God. Her final words were a great testament of her love for Jesus. *"I shall cling to Christ as a burr clings to a coat."*

Lydia of Thyatira

Lydia, the Bible tells us, was a seller of purple cloth. When she heard Paul preach the gospel, the Lord opened her heart. Soon after, she and her household were baptized, making her the first recorded European to convert to Christianity. The conviction the Lord placed on her heart influenced her family to believe in Christ and to be baptized.

God places on our hearts this conviction and uses the gifts he has bestowed upon us to persuade others. Following her baptism, she insisted Paul and his companions stay at her house.

There was no mention of a husband, so we assume she was a widow and a wealthy businesswoman. Lydia's conversion to Christianity, when she had no believing friends or family, took courage. She opened her heart and her home, and it is where the church of Philippi first gathered.

It is believed that Lydia went on to manage and care for the congregation after Paul went on to other Macedonian cities to preach the gospel. "The Lord opened Lydia's heart" (Acts 16:14) and poured out His

Spirit on her just as He poured out His Spirit on the Samaritan woman at the well.

Both these women believed in Jesus and went on to spread the gospel and influenced many others to believe. God chose these women and empowered them with faith and courage to go out and tell everyone about Jesus.

Today, God chooses you too. He wants to pour out His Spirit on you, like He did with Lydia and the Samaritan woman. All you need to do is open your heart to Him and let Him in.

Even on my servants, both men and women, I will pour out my Spirit in those days, and they will prophesy.
Acts 2:18 (NIV)

Monica Of Hippo

Monica was the mother of St. Augustine. She was a faithful and courageous woman who prayed her son into the kingdom of God. She is an example of the power of a praying, faithful mother who tirelessly prays for her children.

Born a Christian, her parents married her to a non-believer. Her husband was a bad-tempered, unfaithful roman who refused her request of baptizing their children. He was annoyed by her prayers to God and her giving to the poor.

Despite all these obstacles, Monica did not waver in her faith. When her husband died, her son Augustine came home, and she discovered he had converted to Manichaeism. This religion had pagan elements and was a rival religion to Christianity. She kicked her son out of her home, and later had a dream that her son, Augustine, would come back to the faith.

From then on, she dedicated her life to praying for him and went searching for him from city to city. She found him in Milan, where they met a local church leader named Ambrose. This encounter had a profound effect on Monica and Augustine's relationship.

After being led astray for seventeen years, Augustine went on to become one of the most influential Christian theologians of all times. Monica never wavered in her dedication and perseverance in waiting for God while He paved the way for St. Augustine.

Monica's persistence had an immeasurable impact on Christianity. She tirelessly prayed for her son, not giving up, and testified to Christ working in his life.

God, in her dream, placed the gift of dedication on Monica's heart for her son's salvation. If you've been gifted with a spirit of dedication, never give up if you sense God's leading. Do not listen to the world and the nay-sayers.

There is a purpose for your life. Jesus will show you the way. Show the same dedication that Monica did. Ask God for strength and your perseverance will pay off.

For I can do everything through Christ, who gives me strength.
Philippians 4:13 (NLT)

Jesus spoke of maternal love as powerful, as powerful as His love for us. In Isaiah 49, He says "Could a woman forget her nursing Child?" "Neither Could I forget you."

Mothers that pray for their children, have the supernatural power to influence their decisions. I pray for my children every day. I see God working in their lives, guiding them, and protecting them from evil.

St. Augustine wrote a book about his mother's undying faith and incessant prayers. In the book "Confessions", he said: *"who wept on my behalf, wept more than most mothers weep when their children die. For she saw that was dead by faith and spirit, which she had from Thee and Thou heardest her, Lord. Thou heardest her and despised not her tears from pouring down. They "watered" the earth under her eyes, in every place where she prayed. You heard her."*

Through her tears and her undying faith, the Holy Spirit poured out of her and spread over the earth. While he was led astray, St. Augustine was dead in spirit. He came to Christ because of the prayers of his mother.

Mary and Martha of Bethany

Mary and Martha were sisters during the time of Jesus' ministry. Lazarus, who Jesus raised from the dead, was their brother. The story of Mary sitting at Jesus' feet while Martha was busy cooking and catering to the guests in her home, shows Mary's dedication and devotion to Jesus.

Martha was preparing the meal for Jesus and the twelve disciples while her sister, Mary, was in discipleship with Jesus. Irritated, Martha asked Jesus, *"Why won't Mary come and help me?"* Jesus responds, *"Martha, you have forgotten the most important thing."*

Jesus loves and rebukes Martha gently, teaching her to have hope and faith like Mary. Martha was so busy working she forgot what really matters, giving Jesus her full attention. Jesus was moved by Mary's quiet devotion numerous times in the Bible.

In Luke 10:38-42, when she chose to sit at his feet while Martha cooked, and in John 11:32-35, when she wept for her brother, Lazarus, Jesus wept with her. He felt her pain and raised Lazarus from the dead. The scripture says Jesus was moved with compassion. Jesus, often, was moved with compassion for the poor in spirit and the needy.

Every time He felt compassion, something wonderful happened. He preached a message, performed a miracle, or stopped and ministered to others in some way. Being compassionate is Christ-like, if you do not naturally have it, you need to cultivate it.

Esther

Perhaps this is the moment for which you have been created.
Esther 4:14

Have you ever wondered what your purpose in life is? Esther discovered her purpose when God chose her to save her people from genocide.

She was an orphaned Jewish girl who was adopted by her older male cousin, Mordecai. She grew up humble and obedient, and accepted her future as the Persian Queen while hiding her Jewish identity.

When her husband signed a decree to kill all the Jewish people in his kingdom, her uncle Mordecai advised her to ask the king to spare her people.

At first, she hesitated out of fear for her life, but Mordecai helped her realize why God chose her to be queen. Mordecai said God planned this before she was born.

Like Esther, you were born for this moment, created for this moment. No matter what you are going through, remember to turn to Him for strength.

Go, gather together all the Jews who are in Susa, and fast for me. Do not eat or drink for three days, night or day. I and my attendants will fast as you do. When this is done, I will go to the king, even though it is against the law. And if I perish, I perish.
Esther 4:16 (NIV)

Esther knew to turn to God for her strength, so she prayed and fasted with her people for three days and waited for God to lead her on how to approach her husband, the king.

She surrendered completely, accepted God's will for her, including possibly death. She trusted God and His plan to use her to save her people. Esther's courage and faithfulness combined with her love for God and for her people saved Israel from annihilation.

Women for thousands of years have contributed to the history of the world. Their faith has influenced many historical events.

These women were known for their great compassion, and they saw people as Jesus saw them. Seeing others in their brokenness, yet still loving them, and feeling compelled to help them.

They did not fear ministering to the poor, and had no fear in proclaiming the gospel, and the Truth of the Word of God.

Your life is precious, and you are ordained by Jesus to go out into the world and make a difference. You hold the key to making the world a better place; to change the world.

Rahab

In the same way, was not even Rahab the prostitute considered righteous for what she did when she gave lodging to the spies and sent them off in a different direction? As the body without the spirit is dead, so faith without deeds is dead.
James 2: 25-26 (NIV)

Rahab, a Canaanite woman living in Jericho, was a prostitute who is a Biblical heroine known for helping the Israelites defeat the pagan city of Jericho.

Before the Israelites crossed the Jordan, they sent out two spies to scout the land. Arriving in Jericho, the men spent the night at Rahab's house. When the King of Jericho heard about the two men, he sent his men to capture them. Rahab hides them and helps them escape.

In return for saving their lives, Rahab and her entire household are spared and become part of the people of Israel. Rahab, then marries Salmon, an Israelite from the tribe of Judah. Joseph, Jesus' earthly father, was a direct descendant of Rahab.

Like the midwives in Egypt who saved Moses, Rahab was faced with fearing God or fearing the ruler of the land. She chose to trust in God when confronted with adversity. In this moment of truth, she defies the King of Jericho and rescues the Israelites. God rewards her and her household with His grace and mercy.

As with Rahab, our past sins are forgiven, and the slate is wiped clean. Rahab is no longer remembered as a prostitute, but as a brave and courageous woman worthy, through God's grace, to be part of the lineage of Christ.

Deborah

Deborah had a unique role in Israel's history. She was an influential female judge, the only female judge mentioned in the Bible in a male-dominated culture. She was a Prophetess who shared God's Word with others. She is known for her wisdom and courage, and it was said she heard God's voice.

She was a warrior, a poet, a singer, and songwriter. Upon receiving instructions from God, she called Barak, another Israelite warrior, to gather 10,000 troops to attack Sisera, Jabin's commander of troops. Barak responded by saying, "If you will go with me, I will go; if not I will not go." Judges 4:8 (NIV) We can learn from her leadership, obedience, courage, and fearlessness. How many of us, in faith, can step out of our comfort zone?

And she said, "I will surely go with you. Nevertheless, the road on which you are going will not lead to your glory, for the Lord will sell Sisera into the hand of a woman." Then Deborah arose and went with Barak to Kedesh.
Judges 4:9 (ESV)

Conclusion

*"But whoever drinks the water I give them will never thirst.
Indeed, the water I give them will become in them a spring of
water welling up to eternal life."*
John 4:14 (NIV)
*Husbands, love your wives, just as Christ loved the church
and gave himself up for her to make her holy, cleansing her
by the washing with water through the word, and to present
her to himself as a radiant church, without stain or wrinkle or
any other blemish, but holy and blameless.*
Ephesians 5:25-27 (NIV)

When Jesus speaks to the Samaritan woman at the
well, he spoke metaphorically of water as salvation.
Water symbolizes the spiritual cleansing that comes
from accepting God's offer of salvation.

God offers salvation and eternal life through faith in
His Son, Jesus Christ. In Ephesians 5:25-27, water is
used to cleanse the bride of Christ, the Church. In the
following verse, Jesus makes the church holy and
blameless "by the washing with water through the
word".

On the last day and greatest day of the feast, Jesus stood and said in a loud voice, "Let anyone who is thirsty come to me and drink. Whoever believes in me, as Scripture has said, rivers of living water will flow from within them."
John 7:37-38 (NIV)

In John, chapter 7 verse 37-38, Jesus declares that those who believe in Him shall have the Holy Spirit flow out of them like "rivers of living water."

Do you thirst for the peace that only comes from a relationship with Jesus? Are you ready to drink the living water from the well? And to have all your sins washed away by divine mercy in the living water of grace?

Are you ready for a cleansed and refreshed spiritual life? To be filled with the Holy Spirit. Are you ready to flood your heart with Living water and to let go of your feelings of shame? To walk with your heart filled with joy knowing that you are loved unconditionally. If you said yes, accept Jesus now as your Savior and drink from the eternal well of salvation.

For you were once darkness, but now you are light in the Lord. Live as children of light (for the fruit of the light consists in all goodness, righteousness and truth) and find out what pleases the Lord. Have nothing to do with the fruitless deeds of darkness, but rather expose them. It is shameful even to mention what the disobedient do in secret. But everything exposed by the light becomes visible—and everything that is illuminated becomes a light. This is why it is said: "Wake up, sleeper, rise from the dead, and Christ will shine on you."
Ephesians 5:8-14 (NIV)

Personal Reflections/Thoughts:

www.ingramcontent.com/pod-product-compliance
Lightning Source LLC
La Vergne TN
LVHW051425080426
835508LV00022B/3240

9 781736 420706